The 90-Minute Guide to Building Marketing Funnels That Convert

Keith Perhac

CEO and Founder of SegMetrics, Inc

The 90-Minute Guide to Building
Marketing Funnels that Convert

Ready to optimize your marketing?
Get free tools to accompany this book at
https://segmetrics.io/bonus/book-funnels-that-convert/

Please send your questions, comments, and feedback to
keith@SegMetrics.io or on twitter at @harisenbon79

ISBN: 9798631971912

To my loving wife Yumiko, and our wonderful daughters, Elena and Alicia. Thanks for putting up with me and giving me perspective as to what's important in both life and business.

Contents

Forward

I've made over $100,000 from the funnels that Keith helped me set up.

If that doesn't get your attention, I don't know what will.

A few years ago, I started building my *Fearless Salary Negotiation* business: I wrote the book, started building a mailing list, set up the website, and made video courses to help people get what they needed quickly since salary negotiations tend to sneak up on people.

I also started working on SEO so more people could find my work when they needed help with job interviews or negotiating job offers. And it worked! More and more people came to my site and read the articles I had published there.

But something was missing. I wasn't *selling* anything to all those visitors. So I reached out to Keith and asked for his help. I knew he had worked with some *really* big businesses and I figured if he could help them, he could probably help me.

"Let's look at your funnels from top to bottom," he said.

And we did. We started with better lead magnets, better Calls To Action (CTAs), better Thank You pages, better nurturing sequences, better sales sequences, better sales pages, and better upsells.

The result?

BETTER SALES. To the tune of more than $100,000 and counting.

That's what funnels are for, right?

And when I read *The 90-Minute Guide to Building Marketing Funnels That Convert*, I saw everything Keith had helped me do with my funnels, distilled into a short little book. It's all there.

Don't let the length fool you: This is the real deal. It's not watered down or "lite"—it's exactly what Keith helped me do to build funnels that turned all that traffic into *sales*.

Do yourself and your business a favor and read this book. Your business will thank you.

Josh Doody
FearlessSalaryNegotiation.com

Introduction

Over the past decade, I've worked with everyone from single-founder startups to Fortune 500s, including Toyota, Circle K, and others.

But the people I enjoy working with most are smaller companies who are looking to grow exponentially in a short time frame.

This has led me to work with some very well-known names in the online world, including Ramit Sethi, Eben Pagan, Andrew Warner Dr. Axe, Jim Kwik, Nomadic Matt, and many others.

Now, a curious thing happened as I worked with these clients...

I quickly discovered how impossibly HARD it was to pull trustworthy, complete, and actionable data out of the existing suite of marketing tools.

How was I supposed to help them optimize their funnels, increase their conversions, and ultimately grow their sales if I couldn't get the "numbers" and data I needed!?

That's what brought me to build SegMetrics - a way to automate getting the accurate numbers that I and other marketers need, so that we can get back the hours and hours of excel and pivot table tasks we do every day, and focus on the marketing that we love so much.

Which leads me to writing to you today.

My mission is to empower you.

To help you transition from the big "launch" model that drains your resources and energy for 3 months at a time every year, and instead move into a more scalable and leveraged model using automated marketing funnels.

I'm here to tell you it's **more than possible** to build an evergreen marketing system that you can plug into paid traffic, and turn those leads into cold hard cash for your business.

That's how you scale. That's how you become far more profitable, while working LESS and having the time to actually work ON your business.

So grab a seat… get comfy… and get ready to completely transform your business for the better.

Yours for more profitable sales funnels,
Keith Perhac

What You'll Learn

I intend this book to be your crash course in sales funnel creation, optimization, and automation.

If that sounds like a mouthful, don't worry!

In about 90 minutes or less, this book will give you the solid foundation you need to start on your journey to automate turning visitors into leads, leads into customers, and customers into raving fans.

Specifically, you'll discover:

- Why automated marketing funnels ARE the bread-and-butter of your business (can you say "goodbye, launch model"?!).

- How optimizing your funnels can lead to a MASSIVE boost in sales (and ultimately, more money in your bank account)

- How you can leverage DATA to make much smarter marketing decisions (that will create far more sales and revenue for your business)

- The 6-step "classic" marketing funnel and how you can implement it in your business

- The three critical things you MUST measure in order to quickly optimize your funnels and get them to convert better

- Why understanding the "Hero's Journey" can be one of the most profitable things you'll ever learn when it comes to email marketing

- And much more…

My goal here is to distill over a decade of in-the-trenches knowledge of creating, deploying, and optimizing funnels into an easy-to-read guide. One that gives you the critical concepts you need to know so you can get started on your journey to higher profits, right away.

I've done my best to start at ground zero, and then slowly build on each chapter, so you can really get the material at a deep level.

It's my hope this opens your eyes and shows you what's

possible when you embrace the technology that's available to marketers and business owners alike.

The days of the once-a-year launch model are numbered. So the sooner you can transition your business to "evergreen" marketing funnels that convert like crazy, the better.

This is where things are headed. And fortunately, it's the key to truly unlocking scale in your business, so you can have the time to work ON your business, instead of running yourself ragged working "in" it (which is all too common with the launch model).

I've done my best to give you everything you need to know to get started on the path. All I ask is that you read the pages that follow with an open mind.

And if there's anything in here you have more questions about or want to learn more, feel free to check out our "Data Beats Opinion" articles at https://segmetrics.io/articles where you can learn more about many of the topics covered here, all for free.

Or shoot me an email at keith@segmetrics.io.

Why I Wrote This Book

I wrote this book because creating an effective marketing funnel can be tough – but it doesn't need to be overwhelming. For over a decade, I've worked with course authors, product creators, and businesses of all sizes to increase their revenue through automated marketing.

In my own experience working with clients of all levels of sophistication, one thing has become clear – there's a certain mindset that's beneficial when designing and improving your marketing funnels.

Once you can get into that "funnel mindset," then designing, measuring and optimizing your marketing funnels becomes infinitely easier.

Throughout this book, I'm going to walk you through getting into that funnel mindset, as well as the ins and outs of building profitable marketing funnels.

You may have just finished your first product launch – at which point you're probably ready for a long nap – or maybe your current marketing funnel isn't performing well and you need to make some changes.

No matter where your business is at, if you have a product or are getting ready to launch one, optimizing your marketing funnels can provide a MASSIVE boost to your bottom line!

But after working with scores of product creators, I've discovered that very few people implement them the right way.

And look… this is not a dig on you or anyone else. I've made plenty of mistakes in the pursuit of a profitable and fully automated marketing funnel.

Making those mistakes is how we improve.

But fortunately for you, I'll teach you the correct way to implement and optimize your marketing.

I'll highlight all of the common mistakes, pitfalls, and misinformation out there, so you can AVOID the mistakes

I made, and many other businesses and marketers continue to make.

And I'll show you the "best practices" for building a wildly successful marketing funnel that works FOR you and your business, now and in the future.

So without further ado… let's get started!

Part 1

Why Marketing Funnels are the Foundation of a Successful Business

As a digital marketer, your marketing funnels form the basis of your business. They are often the main channel your audience interacts with you through, and are the most effective way to sell products at scale.

A marketing funnel describes your customers' journey with you, from the moment they first learn about your business, to the moment that they purchase, and beyond.

Understanding your marketing funnels helps you

understand how to relate to your audience at every stage of their journey with you. Plus, funnels provide a kind of "standard operating procedure" (SOP) for your marketing and sales, and just like any other SOP in your business, the better you define them, the more you can improve them.

Imagine that — an improvable checklist that helps you turn visitors into leads, leads into customers, and customers into evangelists!

In this section, we'll discuss how automating your funnels helps you understand your audience, and improve your marketing.

Funnels help you understand your audience

One of the most overlooked aspects of a marketing funnel is the fact that everyone goes through them at the same pace - but not all at once. Your leads (and customers) go through your funnel over a set period of time.

The beauty of this is that it allows you to set up "touchpoints" throughout your marketing funnels, in order to see how people are engaging with your messaging.

To be clear, what I'm talking about here goes far beyond simple email open and click rates (although those are important!)... and these "touchpoints" can go deeper into what people are looking for as they go through your funnel.

Here's a simple example:

Let's say you decide to send an email to your list asking them a simple question. You ask if they'd be more interested in watching a video targeted at designers or a video targeted at copywriters.

Your subscribers would then click on the option they prefer (a video for designers or one for copywriters).

Now you've got a defined and measurable touchpoint!

You can now see how many people clicked on designer vs. copywriter and get a much clearer understanding of the demographics of your audience.

Touchpoints like these can then be combined with other aspects of your funnel that you're measuring – for example, do leads who identified as *designers* have a higher purchase rate than *copywriters*? Do they open emails more? What about *designers* who attended your webinar?

By looking at how your audience acts throughout your funnel, you understand how different cohorts react to different messaging. Armed with that data, you can now make smarter decisions! In this case, you can now tailor your content towards the underserved cohorts within your audience.

Take for example the *designers* who are thoroughly engaged - they open every email, attend the webinar, but still don't purchase (because what you're offering doesn't apply to them). By measuring the touchpoints in your marketing funnel, you've unearthed a rabid audience that you can create an offer for, instead of just shrugging it off and saying "30% of my audience just isn't interested."

If you hadn't looked at how the *designer* cohort acts compared to *copywriters*, it would be impossible to tell that you had a dedicated fanbase with nothing to buy within your existing marketing.

And while feedback from your customers and audience is always valuable, it's important to understand that people's actions always speak louder than their words. This is why it's so important to define and measure every step of your funnel!

One of the most *visceral* examples of this is the apocryphal urban legend of the yellow Sony Walkman. The story goes that Sony had conducted a focus group to gauge the impressions of their new yellow Walkman.

Sony asked the group their impression of the new yellow Walkman when compared to the existing black one. The results were overwhelming – people loved the sportiness of the yellow one, the bold colors, and the unique design.

However, as the group members left, they were offered the chance to take home either the yellow Walkman or the traditional black one.

Everyone chose the black Walkman.

Actions speak louder than words.

Funnels can be automated

The "killer feature" of a marketing funnel is that it can be automated.

That means you can be on vacation, you can be working ON your business, you can be out sick or just spending time with your friends and family - and your marketing funnel will continue to chug along, turning visitors into leads, leads into customers, and customers into evangelists.

Contrast that to a manual sales process like the traditional launch model. It takes a huge amount of time and energy, and if you're running multiple product launches every year, that time and energy commitment will stifle your ability to grow your business or work on new projects.

Marketing funnels, on the other hand, provide a solution to this "launch churn." That's because they sell your product on autopilot. You just have to take the time to set it up once, and then let it continually sell for you while you focus on improving other aspects of your business.

It's like the old infomercial slogan: "just set it and forget it!"

Rather than developing a new system and flow for each launch, you'll put in the work once to create a killer marketing funnel that you can make changes to over time, to optimize the funnel and increase sales.

A huge benefit that stems from automation is scalability.

Since you aren't limited by your own energy and time, you can sell to a hundred people or a thousand with the same amount of effort. And once you find a source of traffic that constantly turns leads into customers, you can transform your funnel into a killer sales machine.

Additionally, you can automate different paths to take your leads down within your funnel — building segmentation right into the funnel itself.

Different leads can go into different funnels depending on

how they opt in. Since everything is automated, you could even start multiple launches at the same time, giving your prospects a customized experience to what THEY want and are willing to spend money on.

Funnels are like a checklist or SOP for your marketing

As I mentioned earlier, every business has a list of standard operating procedures (SOPs) they abide by, which gives the business identity and establishes a uniform way of doing things.

In the same way, your marketing funnels are a set of steps and processes that turns your visitors into leads, leads into customers, and customers into evangelists.

A well-performing evergreen funnel will give you about a 5% conversion rate to buyer, and that number can grow to 10% or higher with effective optimization.

You can use the fact that these funnels are broken into a series of steps, like a checklist, to your advantage — looking at each point along the process to see where you can improve.

Maybe your fourth email isn't getting opened? Maybe email number six has a low click through rate?

Measuring every step of your funnel like this gives you data, which can then clue you in to where things can be quickly improved.

Funnels allow you to go through each step, make sure everything is performing as expected, and correct course where needed.

Compare this to a launch model, where an email has one chance to make a successful impact. With an automated funnel, every day brings another chance to improve your messaging, and optimize your marketing.

Funnels are the foundation of successful launches and continuous sales

Launching a product is DIFFICULT. Period.

And a huge issue when launching a product is that most of your focus ends up being on the implementation of the strategy, rather than the strategy itself.

I've been a part of hundreds of launches throughout my career. From smaller 6-figure launches, to 8-figure launches — and the one thing that remains constant is the amount of last-minute changes, setup and testing that overwhelms the process.

In a launch, very rarely are we taking extra time on perfecting the strategy — instead, we're just hoping to get the next page up before it goes live in the morning.

When you're first getting started, you might be OK with doing all of the work yourself, from building your product to marketing it to selling it. When it comes time to launch, you've probably ran yourself ragged trying to make as many sales as possible.

But it doesn't matter how successful your initial launch was. What I've seen time and time again, is that profits (and your energy) take a drastic dip once the initial launch is over.

This roller coaster of sales and frantic work defines the traditional launch model, and it's nearly impossible to sustain while trying to grow your business at the same time.

But an effective marketing funnel puts an end to that rollercoaster by selling your product 24 hours a day, 7 days a week, year-round. And get this - it does it with very little to no effort on your part.

This allows you to focus ON the business rather than being constantly stuck IN the business.

With the use of marketing funnels, you'll dramatically raise the ceiling on what your business is capable of when it comes to new launches and igniting a sales engine.

Automated funnels mean less work for you, more time to focus on growing your business, and an automatic source of sales and/or lead generation.

I'll say it again - marketing funnels are the foundation of a successful business!

In the next chapter, we're going to look at one of the key benefits to automated marketing funnels — conversion optimization.

Part 2

- Marketing Funnels are Like a Fine Wine - They Get Better With Age

Probably the biggest benefit of using a marketing funnel is their measurability. Launches and broadcast emails are measurable, but are by their nature, one-off events. It's difficult to segment and test one-off emails, and it's almost impossible to improve them over time.

Marketing funnels, on the other hand, allow you to see where your leads are engaged with your content, and where they lose interest. And because funnels are not one-shot broadcasts, you can use that data to improve your funnels over time.

In this chapter, I'll walk you through a few strategies around measuring and maintaining your marketing funnel, so it keeps getting better and better at converting customers as time goes on.

Measuring how people go through your funnel is key to improving it

Understanding how each individual funnel is performing is the key to improving your marketing. If you only look at your list as a whole, it can be difficult to find the over-performing and under-performing aspects of your marketing strategy.

To take an extreme example, imagine you have one funnel that performs at a 100% conversion rate — which means that everyone who joins the funnel buys your product (who wouldn't love that!). Then, imagine you also have a funnel (with the same number of leads) that has a 0% conversion rate — which means not a single person bought.

Your total conversion rate for your marketing taking both funnels into account is 50% — a respectable number. But imagine if that's all you knew - that your marketing as a whole converts at 50%. You'd probably be happy, but you'd be blind to the fact that you have one amazingly good funnel and one atrociously bad one.

Imagine how much money you'd be leaving on the table by having both funnels running, since you don't know which one is working and which one isn't.

That's why it's so critical to define and measure every step of your funnel *(am I sounding like a broken record yet? Good! Because this is critically important).*

These data points in your funnel are what's known as your Key Performance Indicators (KPIs).

Top-level KPIs measure the health of a business, but disguise your outliers (like the funnel converting at 0% in this example). And when you're looking for places to improve your marketing, **outliers identify places you should work on first.**

This idea of top-level KPIs extends itself to each of your funnels. If you're looking at the overall conversion rate of a funnel (or open rate, or any metric), you see the results, **but not the underlying cause for those actions.**

That's why to understand how to improve your funnel, you need to focus on measuring each **touchpoint** that your leads interact with as they go through your funnel. This allows you to take a semi-abstract concept, like **engagement**, and put a solid conversion and dollar number to it.

The goal that we want to come away with is being able to say with confidence that "People who attend the webinar are twice as likely to convert, and are worth three times as much as people who only watch the replay."

So, how do we measure these touchpoints in our funnel?

In order to identify which touchpoints that your leads are interacting with, we're going to tag them.

(You can also use custom fields for this, and it works just as well, in fact Brennan Dunn at RightMessage recommends using custom fields over tags. For our use case, either is fine, and the strategy is the same.)

How to know what to track?

In the beginning it can be difficult to decide exactly what needs to be tracked in your funnel. In fact, one of the major pitfalls I see is marketers tagging *every* single decision a prospect can make throughout the funnel. While this can be useful if you have good reporting to back it up, most of the time it creates confusion and is more trouble than it's worth.

Instead of tagging every possible decision point, what we need to look at is the actions that a person can take that segment them into one bucket or another.

For example, you don't need to tag people for every blog post they click on during the funnel. Instead, you want to tag for high-impact **decisions** that a prospect needs to make - or for those actions that change how you'll engage with the reader throughout the rest of the funnel.

Remember the example we used earlier? Sending an email to your list and asking whether they wanted a video targeted towards *designers* or *copywriters.*

In this case, them choosing one or the other is an important distinction and action you DEFINITELY want to tag and track. That's because it creates two very different segments in your audience and also changes the way you should market to them based on what they selected (designer vs. copywriter).

I mean, think about it:

You don't want to send copywriters information on color theory, and you don't want to send designers information on why dangling participles aren't the end of the world. (No matter what Mrs. Marsh in 4th grade told you!).

You want to make sure the content you're providing matches the needs of the readers.

Next...

Just as we want to segment people based on *who* they are, we also want to segment people based on *what they do*.

When deciding when to tag people's actions, you should think of those actions like you would a sales funnel – what are the steps that you should watch to see if the work you're doing is having a positive or negative effect.

The classic example of this is a webinar. You'd want to tag people who **register** for the webinar, when they **attend**, if they **stay** for the whole webinar, if they watch the **replay**, and if they ask for a **phone reminder**.

This lets us know not only how many people register and attend each webinar, but also if the phone service increases attendance, and if attending the webinar causes more people to purchase than just watching the replay.

In fact, if we see that the phone reminder and attendance have no bearing on whether people buy or not, we can send everyone to the replay, and use that newly opened space in the funnel to promote content that might convert better.

Make Sure to Check these stats...

Once we have the tracking for our touchpoints set up, we can start looking at how each of them influence the effectiveness of our marketing funnel.

For any touchpoint in the funnel, we want to measure (at least) the following three **KPIs**:

- **Conversion Rate** - Do people who perform the touchpoint convert higher or lower than the average?

- **Lead Value** - Do people who perform the touchpoint generate more or less revenue per lead than the average?

- **Multi-Step Conversion** - In examples like a webinar or sales call, what is the percentage of people who move from one step to the next, and are there steps where people tend to fall out of the funnel?

Once we have these three numbers, we can then start our magic and *combine* different touchpoints, the *who* and the *what*, to see what combinations perform better.

To use our earlier example of designers vs. copywriters, we'd want to know – do *designers* have a higher rate of **webinar attendance** than *copywriters*? And do they have a higher **Lead Value** than the *copywriters* that performed the same actions?

If so, we can try creating a new webinar invite for *copywriters* to increase attendance.

How to Tag Your Marketing Funnel Touchpoints

However you manage and tag your funnel touchpoints, it's important to have a strong naming structure. A good naming structure is critical for mapping out your funnels, and making sure that you can make sense of your marketing years down the road.

A good naming strategy allows you to:

Know what new tags should be named

There is nothing worse than going into your marketing funnels and seeing multiple similarly named tags that you have no idea what they mean. "Affiliates" "affiliate" "aff" could all mean the same thing, or they could be completely different. When you want to mail your affiliates, which one will you use? Having a naming structure prevents duplicate tags from being created, because you'll know just where to look to see if a tag already exists.

Grouping Similar Segments

A predefined naming structure also allows you to quickly find cohorts and segments that are similar to each other. If all your social leads have the phrase "social" in them, you can quickly identify those leads. Similarly, if you tag users by profession with the "profession - designer" tag, you can quickly get a list of all the professions and how they convert in any given funnel.

Noting Tag Purpose

Tags can have different jobs, and sometimes you may want to remove tags (for example, to stop a campaign, or remove access to a product) but still be able to see what actions a contact has taken for analytics. For example, if we apply the "Member - VIP Community" to give people access to our membership site, we need to remove that tag when they leave the community. That would prevent us from getting a list of all people who were ever in the community. Instead, we'd want to use an additional tag like "Historical - Member - VIP Community" that is never removed, so that we can separate the reporting of that touchpoint from the business use of giving someone access to the product.

Segmenting Cohorts or Campaigns

Likewise, prefixing your campaign tags with a unique identifier is an effective way to create "campaign reports" of every step that leads take when going through your funnel.

Let's dive into that campaign segmentation a little deeper.

Following a campaign segmentation strategy lets you understand where people are coming into your marketing from, what they've experienced, and finally what makes them purchase. And it does this in a way that lets you track the effectiveness of your campaigns - days, months, even years after your contacts have gone through them.

This also allows you to create a "Campaign Report" that breaks down contacts by tag prefix. So if you use a consistent naming structure for your campaign tags, you can easily see how each step of your funnel affects your lead value, and sales revenue.

Here's an example of what a campaign looks like:

Name	Leads	Cust	Conv	Sales	Value
30-Day Nurture: Start	5,792	97	1.67%	$9,991	$1.72
30-Day Nurture: Completed	3,038	97	3.19%	$9,991	$3.29
30-Day Nurture: Active	2,754	0	0%	$0	$0
30-Day Nurture: Download PDF	2,985	46	1.54%	$4,738	$1.59
30-Day Nurture: Webinar Register	2,618	51	1.95%	$5,253	$2.01
30-Day Nurture: Webinar Attend	1,617	51	3.15%	$5,253	$3.24
30-Day Nurture: Purchase	97	97	100%	$9,991	$103

As we can see, it's profitable to get people to attend the webinar.

Now, let's look at how we can organize our tags with a naming structure that will help you create a campaign report to better understand how people flow through your marketing funnel, and find which touchpoints cause them to convert into customers.

The following campaign tagging structure is a recommendation based on years of optimizing marketing funnels. This is not the only way to track leads through your marketing, but it does cover a number of edge cases and issues that I've seen working on thousands of marketing campaigns.

If you already have your own tagging structure, *excellent!*

Don't feel like you need to tear everything out and use this one. Pick and choose, going through the guide to see which tags you may need to add to your existing structure to better optimize your flow.

Let's get started!

Campaign Tagging Guide

For each campaign, there are 6 **required** tags to track people through the funnel, and then a number of **optional** tags that you can use to track the various **touch points** as people go through the campaign.

Required Tags

- **seq- {campaign name}: Start**: Applied to all contacts who go through the funnel. This tag will be the main tag we look at when judging the lead-generation ability of the funnel.

- **seq - {campaign name}: Completed**: Applied to everyone at the end of the funnel (whether they purchase or not). This tag will be the main tag we look at when judging the profitability of a funnel, as anyone with this tag will have completed the funnel.

- **seq - {campaign name}: Active**: Shows people who are currently in the funnel. It should be removed at the end of the funnel.

- **In active campaign:** This tag signifies whether a lead is currently going through one of your funnels, and often used to remove people from other funnels or newsletters while they are going through a funnel. *It should be removed at the end of the funnel.*

- **seq - {campaign name}: Purchase**: If the contact purchases from this funnel, tag them to delineate from purchases they might have made through other places on the site.

- **seq - {campaign name}: Origin**: This tag is applied only if this is the first campaign that the contact goes through. It's set to show which campaigns bring in the most people, and are the most effective at long-term conversions

Optional Tags

In addition to the 6 required tags above, it's recommended that you use campaign-specific versions of your tags to measure the effectiveness of various touch points throughout your funnel.

Some examples of these might be:

- seq - {campaign name}: Download PDF

- seq - {campaign name}: Webinar - Register

- seq - {campaign name}: Reply Email

- seq - {campaign name}: Completed Survey

- seq - {campaign name}: Downsell - {product name}

- seq - {campaign name}: Upsell - {product name}

Part 3

-You're Not Your User-
Looking at Your
Funnel for the First
Time

One of the biggest mistakes that we as marketers make is forgetting that your leads are going through your funnel for the *very first time*. We see the funnel as a whole, and we know the end game; but we forget that the people going through it only see one step at a time — the moment that they're in.

This can lead to us second-guessing ourselves, and falling into a number of common pitfalls that prevent us from creating the best experience for our leads. Part of the *Expert's Dilemma* means that it's hard for us to put ourselves in the shoes of our audience — who are learning all this for the first time. But it's necessary in order to effectively nurture our leads into customers.

In this chapter, we'll go over many of the common mistakes and misconceptions when it comes to creating marketing funnels so you can avoid them in your business.

Mistake #1: Believing you're emailing too much

One of the most common mistakes that marketers make is believing they are emailing their list **too much**. It's easy to feel that way, because we see all the emails laid out in front of us, and we're reminded of the hundreds of emails we get every day.

But that's approaching the question from the wrong angle.

Instead of focusing on the quantity of the emails you send, focus on the quality of the emails you send!

The fact of the matter is: **if your emails are providing**

engaging information, and real value, there's no need to worry about emailing too much.

So stop worrying if three or four emails is too much for one week. Focus on creating value-packed content for every single email.

Mistake #2: Selling too much!

Another extremely common mistake is marketers and business owners selling to their list, way too often.

Think of it this way: someone giving you their email address is already a transaction. They've already bought something from you. The only difference being that instead of paying you with money, they've given you access to their inbox.

This is a transaction that you have to believe has value — because the people on your list definitely do.

Over-selling is especially problematic for cold leads - that is, people who are visiting your site for the first time. Trying to sell them again right out of the gate is a sure-fire way for them to hit the unsubscribe button. It's not the way you want to start your relationship.

(Note that this only applies to emails – a tripwire offer on a landing page, or a one-time-offer after getting their email address is a great strategy to increase revenue)

Instead of harping on the constant sale, you should focus on emailing frequent, educational and value-driven content… especially within the first two weeks of subscribing.

Remember that you only get one chance at a first impression. Your initial emails will set the tone for how your new leads see you the rest of their time with you. Focusing on content, value, and education sets you apart as a trusted resource for valuable content, versus just another salesperson.

A good rule of thumb is that at least **two-thirds** of the emails you send out should be educational content. No selling whatsoever.

By doing this, you'll build a reputation of providing value first, which makes it much easier to ask for a sale further down the road.

Mistake #3: Sending broadcasts to leads going through a funnel

Following along with Mistake #2, it's critical that you separate people who are going through your marketing funnel from your main broadcasts.

That's because you want your marketing funnel to be self-contained – you can't measure the success of the funnel if the leads going through it are getting daily or weekly emails, or even other offers that you're sending out on your broadcast emails.

Your broadcast emails generally assume that someone has been on your list, and knows who you are – whereas your initial marketing funnels are generally leading people through a set narrative to educate them about who you are and the value of your products.

Sending out funnel emails and broadcasts simultaneously would be similar to reading the Lord of the Rings, and then every couple of pages have a page from Twilight stuck in there.

"Look to my coming, at first light, on the fifth day. At dawn, look to the… About three things I was absolutely positive. First, Edward was a vampire. "

Umm, NO….

Mistake #4: Sending everyone through your funnel at once

One of the main advantages of marketing funnels is that you can tweak different steps of the process in order to refine the funnel and maximize sales. If there's an email with a low open rate, you can improve the subject line. Or maybe people are constantly replying with the same question. Now you can add it to one of the emails early on to overcome their objections.

Since the ability to improve your funnel over time is a core feature, you don't want to send your entire list through your funnel at once!

Start with small segments of your list and measure the performance of each spot along the funnel so you can tweak and refine for future iterations. You'll see that different segments go through your funnels in different ways, and respond to emails differently.

This will help you build out the touchpoints in your funnel to identify which segments should get which emails, and how each responds to different offers.

After working as a Japanese Salaryman for over a decade, I became intimately aware with the business philosophy known as Kaizen.

Kaizen, or "improvement," states that small, continuous improvements to a system will yield compounded results.

Your marketing funnel is the same.

Making small improvements regularly eventually compound - creating massive results (conversions and sales).

That's why it's important to not send everyone on your list through your funnel at once. You won't know where you need to improve until it's too late!

Mistake #5: Prematurely optimizing your funnel

One of the major benefits of online marketing is that you can measure pretty much every interaction that a person has with your company. It's something we often take for granted, but the ability to see where visitors came from, which emails they opened, and how far they read on our sales pages is the holy grail of marketing analytics.

This is especially true when we look at our funnels.

However, without an understanding of how a marketing funnel works, it can be tempting to prematurely optimize the wrong parts of your funnel.

Back in my consulting days, I had a number of clients who would want to optimize their sales page, because they weren't getting enough sales. *A worthy endeavor!* Optimizing your sales page is a sure-fire way to increase sales.

The problem? **They only had 3 people see that sales page a week.**

If we were to focus on optimizing the sales page, it would take months, or even years, before we could get enough traffic to see if our changes had improved sales or not.

We needed to get more people to the sales page.

Which meant that we needed to get more people to click on the email.

Which meant that we needed to get more people to **open** the email.

I think you can see where I'm going with this.

When optimizing: **Start with the step that has the worst conversion rate, closest to the top of the funnel.**

Not only is the top of the funnel easier to optimize than the bottom, without enough traffic, you won't be able to know if you're actually optimizing anything, or just throwing darts in the dark.

Which brings me to …

Mistake #6: Missing the truth behind the numbers

Many of the conversion numbers we see in our funnel are straightforward — conversion rate for a sales page, for instance, lets us know how good our copy and positioning is. Our webinar attendance shows us how good we were at reminding people that a webinar was going live.

But there are three numbers that are *crucial* to a marketing funnel that have had their meanings blurred. And it's understandable that people misunderstand the significance of these numbers, as even most CRMs don't create a clear distinction in meaning.

Each email that you send out is a three-step funnel, all in of itself — and each of these steps needs to be optimized separately, as they each rely on the previous step.

Let's break these steps down one by one:

The first step is **Deliverability**: how good of a reputation that your sending domain has and how many of your emails got where they were going. This is influenced by a number of factors that are beyond your control, but making sure your settings are correct, and that you are sending out your mail to a list that is regularly cleaned will help immensely.

If your emails are not being delivered, they can't go to the next step:

The second step is your email's **Open Rate**: how many people opened your email.

This seems straight-forward, but many people attempt to improve the body copy of emails with low open rates. After deliverability, **there is only one aspect of the email that will affect your open rate**. And that is your subject line.

Improving your subject line is key to increasing conversion in your funnel, as it doesn't do much good to have amazing content that no one opens because of a boring subject line!

The final step is looking at the email's **Click Through Rate (CTR)**: how many people clicked on a link in your email. This tells you the quality of the body copy of the email. Was it engaging enough that it compelled someone to click on your offer?

But... Most email systems calculate CTR based on the number of emails sent — not the number of people who opened the email. Which doesn't help if your email has a low open rate, as those numbers can become skewed quickly.

That's why you should measure the Open/CTR ratio! That is, figure out how many people clicked on your links in your email. Then divide that by the number of people that actually *opened* your email.

These measurements will give you an idea of how engaging your content is, and if there are emails or subject lines that need refining!

Remember, it's all about quality when it comes to emailing your subscribers. If what you send is truly valuable, people will read it.

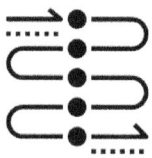

Part 4

- Your Funnel
At a Glance -
The Classic 6-Step
Marketing Funnel

Now that we understand the importance of a marketing funnel, as well as the high-level business goals, we're going to go through a tried-and-true "classic" 6-step sales funnel. This serves as a great jumping off point, and works extremely well over a ton of different markets and industries.

It is a solid performer and a fantastic place to start when building your evergreen funnel.

We call it "classic" because it hits all the points that a sales funnel should have, but doesn't mix in too many complicated strategies.

This funnel acts as a starting point for you to tweak and customize to suit your audience and marketing style. However, keep in mind that each step feeds into the next, and each touchpoint is an opportunity to increase the dollar value of each lead in your funnel.

Even though this is a classic funnel, it's amazing how many companies focus on only **one** part of the funnel, completely forgetting that it's the combination of all the aspects of the funnel that makes it so effective.

In this part, we'll lay out the fundamental aspects to a well-performing funnel, and then go into detail of each step in the following parts of this book.

Step 1: The Optin Magnet

The first step of your funnel is your optin magnet.

An optin magnet entices readers to give you their email address in exchange for something valuable.

There are a number of different tools to set this up and collect emails on your website such as SumoMe or LeadPages, but the most critical part is the **offer** that you make.

It's not enough to say, "Hey give me your email address because I'm great!"

Remember, people value their email address.

You have to offer something valuable in exchange for a precious seat in their email inbox!

Your offer could be anything! A PDF checklist, an eBook, a mini course, a discount of some sort… just so long as it provides value that the reader is looking for.

I find that optin magnets that give people immediate, actionable information (like checklists, webinars, quizzes) are some of the post effective ways to get people on your list.

We'll go into more detail on how to design your optin magnet in Part 5: Turning Visitors into Leads.

Step 2: Offer For More Info (Bigger Ask) or One-Time Offer (OTO)

Immediately after someone gives us their email address, we

want to follow up with a slightly bigger offer. After submitting the opt-in form, people are in a YES frame of mind. We want to use that power of saying YES to continue on and ask for a bigger commitment.

This is the same psychology that makes post-purchase upsells so effective. Once someone has said yes to a purchase, they are more likely to say yes again. That's how McDonalds gets you to super-size your meal, and how Best Buy gets you to buy the extended warranty. (We'll go into more detail on upsell psychology in Part 8)

In this case, we're going to ask for one of two things:

1. We ask for a deeper commitment to the list (like signing up for a webinar), or…

2. We ask for a small one-time purchase (sub $50), and make it a one-time-offer that they'll never see again.

We generally see that a sub $50 product, offered as a one-time-offer on the thank-you page has a 2% conversion rate. This has been fairly consistent over a number of our clients, in a variety of industries.

Step 3: Educational, Warming Funnel

Now that people are on your list, the next part of the funnel is a sequence of emails that presents a narrative mimicking the hero's journey. The Hero's Journey is a narrative practice coined by Joseph Campbell, and is the foundation for many of the myths and stories that have become classics in our society.

It also works amazingly well as a marketing narrative.

Who knew?

We'll go over the full hero's journey email sequence in Part 7, but I want to give a preview of it here.

The hero's journey provides educational value in the form of a story. You'll speak about an example hero (either yourself or a past customer) and how he or she overcame the problem(s) that your audience is experiencing, using a particular method.

It takes the reader from where they are to where they want to be, through the story of someone just like them — creating an emotional connection to the content.

The reason it works so well is because It's one thing to say that your particular product/service/method is great or the best. It's an entirely different (and more powerful) thing to show that it works great through the story of someone else's success!

Step 4: Sales Funnel

So now that you've taken your readers through the hero's journey, showing that people just like them have overcome the same problems, issues and roadblocks, it's time to make your offer!

These emails will offer the exact solution or method that your heroes used in the hero's journey sequence to overcome their obstacles. Because your readers are primed from the previous sequence, they'll be far more likely to buy from you than if you had just made a cold offer!

One important aspect to remember about the sales portion of the funnel is that there needs to be some urgency attached. This can be created through a discount, bonus content, or simply selling a product that is not normally available.

Adding scarcity to the offer prevents people from procrastinating on making a buying decision, and forces them to draw a line in the sand about whether they want the product or not.

We'll go over the sales funnel in much more detail in Part 7!

Step 5: Upsell/Downsell

At this point in the funnel, it's time to pick up some extra revenue or help people who are sitting on the fence cross the finish line.

We'll start with upsells. You should always have an extra or bonus that you offer to people who purchase your product. This goes back to keeping readers in the YES mindset that we talked about earlier.

We'll talk more about upsell strategy in Part 8, but we have worked on funnels where the upsell ended up providing MORE THAN HALF the revenue of the entire funnel. They're that effective.

As for downsells, these should be used for readers who engaged in the funnel, but for whatever reason did not buy. This offer is usually a lite version of your product or a cheaper product that is thematically similar to the main product you are selling.

This helps people who aren't fully convinced of the value of the product to start at a lower commitment level.

Step 6: Last Chance Offer

Finally, about a week or two after the launch has ended, you'll want to send one or two emails to readers who still haven't purchased, where you can present a last-chance offer to collect more sales.

This offer should be the same product as was offered during the regular sales funnel. So, if your funnel is selling your $1000 product for $500, this last chance offer should also be for $500.

We'll be going over the tactics to move more customers over the finish line in much more detail in Part 9!

So there you have it: a sales funnel that will see success in almost any industry or niche! This powerful funnel will be the foundation of your evergreen marketing for your products, and with its implementation, you are going to see your sales increase.

Now, you can absolutely modify this funnel to your specific situation, if it makes sense. But remember, each section of the funnel you remove decreases your ability to generate sales.

They don't call it "tried and true" for nothing!

Part 5

Turning Visitors into Leads

You've heard the story of the carrot and the stick, right? It goes something like this:

A boy hitches up his donkey to a cart, but the obstinate donkey won't pull it down the road. Hitting the donkey with a stick doesn't solve the problem (and it isn't very nice, either). So, the boy ties a carrot to the stick and dangles it in front of the donkey's nose, and – bingo. It's happy to pull the cart all day in hopes of reaching that carrot.

How does this apply to your marketing funnel?

Just like the donkey, your visitors need something enticing — a carrot — before they'll do what you want them to do - in this case, become leads for your product or service.

That's why in this chapter, we'll talk about how to create an enticing "carrot," and how to make sure that your offer ties into the product you'll sell in your marketing funnel.

In this case, your marketing funnel starts with dangling a "carrot" - which is the optin magnet we talked about earlier.

You want it to be something the prospect really wants and speaks to their current pain or problem. For example, if someone had back pain, a free report detailing " 3 Simple Exercises You Can Do At Home To Eliminate Low-Back Pain For Good!" would be an effective carrot.

Another consideration is to make sure that your optin magnet dovetails with the main product your funnel is selling.

A simple way to know if this is the case would be if your optin magnet converts visitors into leads effectively, but then those leads aren't buying what your funnel is selling.

For example, if you followed up the "Eliminate Low-Back Pain" carrot with "Composting for Fun and Profit," you probably won't get many sales. There's a disconnect between the carrot and the offer.

If this is the case, you'd have to either change up your product, or create a different lead magnet that attracts a better-qualified lead for your product.

Now, when it comes to coming up with an idea for your optin magnet, it's good to ask yourself two simple questions:

"What is the quickest win you can give your leads that provides real value?"

"What can you do to help make that shareable?"

One thing we've found is that while PDF checklists are nice to have, our best results have come from offering free assessments (to the tune of 60% optin rates for organic traffic!).

That's because assessments are easy to fulfill and give real value. Plus, they can be as complex or as simple as you want.

They're also personal, are infinitely shareable, and are great for traffic sources like SEO and PPC alike.

But ultimately, go with whatever optin magnet makes the most sense for your business and target audience.

So long as it's valuable and something your visitors WANT,

then you'll be golden and well on your way to building a high-converting funnel.

What are the components of a tasty carrot?

So it's one thing to just tell you to create something valuable. But I want to make 100% sure you know how to create a "tasty" carrot your target audience loves.

After all, this is the first critical touchpoint in your funnel. If you don't get this part right, then the rest doesn't matter.

That said, let's take a look at the components of a high-converting optin magnet (carrot):

Relevant: The content reinforces your course themes or ideas.

Short: You're not giving away your whole product, just a taste.

Easily digestible: Your customer can understand the content without much effort or expertise.

Widely appealing: It speaks to a broad range of potential customers and isn't too narrowly focused.

High quality: It's well designed and on brand, representing the best of what you have to offer.

Instantly actionable: Your customer can benefit from this information right here, right now.

Some more examples of great carrots to get you thinking...

You're marketing a course about how to close sales. As a carrot, you offer a cold-call email script that customers can use verbatim.

You're marketing a course about becoming a more effective blogger. Your carrot is a 10 point checklist that helps you write better blog titles.

You're marketing a course about how to build the house of your dreams. You provide a worksheet with questions that you can use when interviewing potential contractors.

Makes sense, right?

You get someone's email address, they get some quality, helpful content. Everybody's happy.

Importance of Ad / Offer Fit

Another important point to mention when it comes to your optin magnet, is that you want to provide a seamless and **relevant** experience from start to finish.

Which means that the ad you use to get people to your optin page needs to be relevant in all ways to your "offer" for your optin magnet.

That means using similar words, the graphics should look similar, etc.

What you don't want is a disconnect - where the prospect is expecting one thing after clicking on your ad, and then lands on an optin page that looks and feels totally different.

So make sure your ad is in line with your optin magnet.

If your optin magnet is about solving lower-back pain, then your ad should be about lower-back pain as well and use the same or similar images, company logo, etc.

I can't stress the importance of this enough.

Keep this in mind when writing ads to get traffic to your optin!

Understanding that an Email Address has Value

I've already harped on this a little bit earlier, but it bears repeating:

A visitor's email address is VERY valuable.

Remember that a stranger giving your business their email address is essentially a transaction. But instead of dollars and cents, the currency is permission to email that person in the future.

That's why it's so important to treat every aspect of this "transaction" with your optin magnet with the care and attention to detail it deserves.

I'll give you an example of what I mean...

I'm a huge fan of 37signals, a company that provides software as a service (SaaS) products like Basecamp.

They generally do things right.

But in one instance, they were offering an optin magnet - their bestselling book "Getting Real."

The "deal" was that in exchange for giving them your email address, you would get this bestselling book for free.

That's a win-win for everyone – subscribers get a great book jam-packed with software development goodness, and 37signals increases their exposure.

Good deal, right?

But here's where they slipped... 37signals presented this digital copy of a physical 'dead tree' bestselling book that sells for $25 in bookstores across the country like this:

"GET THE FREE PDF"

Calling their book a "free PDF" commoditized the information inside and stripped away almost every last drop of value.

People were questioning its worth, amounting it to a collection of old information gathered from the internet.

Nobody wants a PDF, even if it's identical to a bestselling book.

While 37signals hasn't released any numbers, we're willing to bet that the opt-in rates suffered by the low perceived value of their offer. How you present your product has a big effect on how it's perceived.

So make sure to put it in the best light, even if you're giving it away for free. Because what you're asking for in return - a visitor's email address - has tremendous VALUE.

Optin / Funnel Fit

Don't Go Overboard to Start - Iterate and Improve

Another consideration when building out the initial start of your funnel (the optin magnet) is to ensure there is a "fit" between the optin and the rest of your funnel.

Going back to our back-pain example, if someone opts in to receive a guide showing them three exercises to relieve back-pain, don't have the rest of the funnel talk about how to solve knee pain.

You want to keep things relevant from start to finish. This is how you maximize conversions.

So in our lower back-pain example, the rest of the funnel can be about how there is a specific method or technique to eliminating not only lower back-pain, but all kinds of back-pain.

To a visitor who opted in because they have back pain, this would be relevant and something they'd be interested in learning more about.

So keep this in mind as you build out the rest of your funnel - make sure every piece makes sense and is part of a greater whole.

That said, don't worry about going too deep at first.

Yes, you want to maintain relevance throughout your funnel.

But squash the urge to want to go overboard at the

beginning and make everything PERFECT.

The goal here is to implement and then iterate and improve.

So mission #1 is to get your funnel up and running using the "best practices" we're discussing here.

Once you have data, then you can go to each of the touchpoints and improve one at a time.

Part 6

Why Educational Funnels are Vitally Important
(and Why Most of Them SUCK)

Let's get one thing clear: you MUST stand out from the sea of generic emails that exist out there if you want to have success with your online business.

After all, your prospects don't know you from Adam… so you have to give them a reason to invest their time and energy into consuming your content, and eventually, buying your products or services.

So what's the best way to do that?

Drum roll, please…

Education.

The more you can educate and be entertaining at the same time, the better.

By educating your prospects through your emails, you are by definition providing value. That's because your prospect is now more knowledgeable about their challenge/problem than they were before they met you.

Next, educating positions you as an authority on the subject. This creates trust, which is a must-have if you're going to sell someone something, right?

That's why we're going to dive deep on how to do that with your funnel. It's the best way to take someone who doesn't know you, and getting them to buy your product or service.

In this chapter, I'm going to show you why educational funnels are critical to building a profitable marketing funnel, as well as some tips on how to stand out from the generic email crowd. In order to stand out, you need to make three things clear right from the get-go:

1) Who you are!

It might sound obvious, but the first step in your educational funnel is to introduce yourself. Remember, you're building a relationship, so don't hide behind a website or blog. Make a personal connection with your reader right from the start.

People connect with people more than they connect with companies. That's why so many companies create a spokesperson (like Dave from Wendy's) in order to create a connection with their customers.

A recurring theme that you'll see throughout this book is *the more people can relate to you, the more they will trust you.*

2) Why should anyone listen to you?!

You have to make it clear why people should listen to what you have to say! You can list your accomplishments, give case studies, or show why you are an authority in a particular area.

But don't stress if you don't have a long list of credentials. Oftentimes, people just need to know that you've solved a problem before, and you've helped a few other people do it too.

In fact, telling your own story about how you overcame obstacles is a great way to get others to realize that you know what you're talking about – because you've lived through the same pain they're trying to overcome.

We'll get to that more in Part 7: the Hero's Journey.

3) What value are you going to provide?!

Last but not least, you have to tell your reader what value you're going to provide. What is the problem you are going to help them solve? What is the obstacle you are going to help them overcome?

Make this clear so they stay tuned in to what you have to say.

These are the key things you need to get people to connect with you and stay engaged on your email list.

But getting people on your list is just the first step. Then you have to actually deliver.

You have to make sure you provide the content that they opted in for.

If someone signed up for a PDF list of the best gluten-free hot sauces, don't give them a recipe for how to make cheesecake!

I see a lot of businesses dangle an attractive carrot, but then completely fail to deliver on their promise. This is an easy way to collect a lot of unsubscribes! Remember that your readers giving you their email address was the first step in a transaction. **You now have a responsibility to deliver on that initial promise, or you'll lose that trust and engagement.**

The first thing you want to focus on in your funnel is to deliver quality, informative, content. The first 1-2 weeks of an effective funnel are absolutely critical, and a huge opportunity for you to set things off on the right foot.

And, like I explained in Part 3, don't be afraid of emailing too much during this initial period! You don't want to collect their email and just disappear, because you'll be forgotten and your subscribers will question why they signed up in the first place.

Give your list solid, quality, educational content and you'll build an engaged following that is interested in opening every email.

Don't Sell!

Remember: an educational funnel is NOT a place for you to sell. It's your opportunity to begin building a relationship with the reader, by providing real, valuable information.

And just like the name implies, make sure to actually teach something! This isn't the place to just talk about yourself and how great you are. Offer actionable bits of information or tips that can be implemented quickly, so your readers can start to see results.

Prime the Pump

One thing that a number of marketers and business owners forget to do with their sales funnels is to PRIME THE PUMP.

Unless people are intimately aware of the problem you're solving, you'll need to introduce them to (a) the problem, and (b) what hurdles that problem creates for them.

You want your education funnel to establish a problem mindset and prime the pump for the reader.

That means, for the full duration of this funnel, the problem your readers are facing is first and foremost on their mind. As they keep reading your emails, they think more and more about the problem(s) they're facing in their own lives.

This is so important because, by the time you actually offer something for sale, they are practically begging for a solution to the problem! They've thought about it so much and will reach a breaking point where they have to take action.

A great example of this would be a product that helps people solve gut-biome issues. You might be saying, "what the heck is a gut-biome?" That's exactly what I said when I first heard of them.

I primed the pump myself, by learning all I could about it. I started learning how the gut-biome is the totality of all the bacteria and other microorganisms that live in your intestines. Then I became aware of how a lot of the stomach problems, and low energy issues I was having could be caused by an imbalance in my gut-biome.

Now I have solid information that explains a potential cause of what I've been feeling, and I've identified things that I can do to start feeling better, and researching on my own.

The pump is primed for me to be presented with a solution to my problem.

Why aren't people buying in the first 7 days!?

Once you've established your educational funnel and people receive a few emails that deliver great content, then you can finally offer something for sale.

This is where the lion's share of sales will come.

HOWEVER ...

Not everyone will buy right then and there.

And it's totally OK if you don't make a sale on your first try, or even your second or your third.

If you're presenting high quality content that educates, you'll be creating fans who have the potential to turn into buyers later.

Don't neglect these people! I often see marketers completely stop caring about folks who didn't buy the first time, and that's a huge mistake.

In fact, for cold traffic, your lead value will generally see a huge jump after the 30 or 60-day mark. One client we work with was seeing $1.80 lead value after 14 days. Not terrible but not great either. But those same leads, after 60 days were worth over $5 per lead.

In 6 weeks, the value of those leads essentially tripled!

Sometimes it takes a little longer for someone to be convinced that what you're selling is the real deal – and those are usually the people who are going to be your best customers in the long term.

Play the long game. Don't be obsessed with the quick sale. The payoff will be well worth it.

Now that we understand how valuable educating our prospects through our funnel can be, we'll dive in next into the Hero's Journey … and show you how you can use this monomyth to craft an educational and engaging email sequence that will have customers begging to buy.

Part 7

- Winter is Coming - Warm Cold Leads with the Hero's Journey

The hero's journey is a narrative pattern that appears over and over again in stories across a variety of cultures and time periods.

Joseph Campbell was a scholar who noticed this pattern, and coined it the "hero's journey."

It describes the archetype of the hero who ventures out on a journey where he or she overcomes adversity in order to achieve an ultimate goal.

That's the gist of it, but Joseph Campbell has actually broken up the hero's journey into 12 different stages, each one serving an important purpose.

Some examples of the hero's journey in popular fiction would be timeless stories like Star Wars and The Lord of the Rings!

In this chapter, we're going to learn why the hero's journey is such a fantastic template for your evergreen funnel.

The Hero's Journey

Now, the first question you might be asking yourself is:

"What on earth does this have to do with sales and marketing funnels!?"

Well, by using the hero's journey as the structure of your educational email sequence, you have the ability to take readers on a journey from where they are to where they want to be!

Remember: People don't buy your product because they want the product itself. They want to be better people and solve their problem or challenge. **The product you offer is**

simply a tool that gets them where they want to be.

Now, the reason the hero's journey works so well is that narratives and stories are very powerful forms of marketing. They are easy for us to remember and latch onto emotionally.

This is one of the reasons that Malcolm Gladwell is such an influential author. He takes statistics and weaves the information into a narrative, which makes them all the more convincing and digestible.

Ironically, statisticians and researchers generally hate his books because they gloss over too many important variables and the results are often "spurious." However, most people love his books because he takes complicated analysis and wraps it in an easily understandable narrative that we can emotionally connect to.

I don't want to debate the morals of Malcolm's strategy & writing, but there is no denying its efficiency by connecting with the reader by providing a strong narrative.

This is what we want to do in your marketing funnels.

Overcoming Adversity

The hero's journey is all about overcoming adversity. Right

now, your potential customers are facing some sort of problem in their life or business that you have the solution to..

By taking them through the hero's journey narrative, you inspire them to take action and show them it's actually possible to begin their own journey towards solving that problem! (Usually, by following your advice, and purchasing your product)

It's important to understand that you are not wasting time by taking your readers through a 10-12 email hero's journey educational funnel – you are building a foundation for engagement.

In each email, you're continually re-introducing the issue that you plan to solve with your product, and you continue to "prime the pump" with every email you send.

Who is the Hero?

Now, in order for the hero's journey to work, you need, well, a hero!

You can star as the hero or it can be someone you've helped in the past… or both! It really doesn't matter.

The important thing is to tell the story in the format of the hero's journey.

Though one caveat:

DO NOT MAKE UP A STORY.

Use yourself if you have to. If you can't use yourself, find someone who undertook a journey to overcome the same or a similar obstacle.

What is important is that this hero is authentic and relatable. You want your readers to see themselves in the hero. Make sure that the hero starts from somewhere that your readers can relate to.

If your readers are all working class, "pull ourselves up by the bootstraps" kind of people, don't use a billionaire trust-fund heir to an oil-baron fortune as your main hero – they won't relate.

Use someone who started out at the bottom, and WORKED THEIR WAY UP to be an oil baron.

Make sense?

The story needs to fit who your audience is. It needs to be relevant to THEM.

Applying the Hero's Journey to your Email Sequence

So let's dive into how you can apply the Hero's Journey to your email sequence.

Here are the 12 stages of the Hero's Journey as documented by Joseph Campbell:

1. Ordinary World
2. Call to Adventure
3. Refusal of the Call
4. Meeting the Mentor
5. Crossing the Threshold
6. Tests/Allies/Enemies
7. Approach to the Inmost Cave
8. Ordeal
9. Reward (Seizing the Sword)
10. The Road Back
11. Resurrection
12. Return with the Elixir

You'll notice how familiar these steps are. Think back to any fantasy movie you've watched or book you've read, and you'll find that the story goes through each of these 12 stages.

You want the same thing in your emails.

For example, for step 1 - ordinary world - you want to show how you were just an ordinary guy or gal, going about life, just like your readers. And you also shared the same problem or challenge they have right now.

Then, in step 2 - call to adventure - you can talk about how you were sick and tired of the problem and committed to figuring it out come hell or high water.

Then in step 3 - refusal of the call - you might talk about how your efforts came up short and you were going to throw in the towel until …

In step 4 - meeting the mentor - you came across this weird "trick" you'd never heard of before that could quickly solve your problem. You were skeptical, but intrigued…

And so on and so forth.

If you're interested in learning more about the Hero's Journey, I highly recommend checking out Joseph Campbell's book, *The Hero with a Thousand Faces*. It's a fascinating read and will give you a really good understanding of what you want your email sequence to accomplish in terms of the hero's journey.

Auxiliary Content

Another important point when crafting your hero's journey emails, is that you want to include auxiliary content.

This can take the form of links to extra resources at the end of certain emails that provide extra value and handle objections your audience may have head on.

Some examples for auxiliary content could be:

- A PDF Worksheet

- An in-depth blog post on a topic from an email

- A supplemental video

These auxiliary pieces of content also serve to strengthen the connection between your prospect and you. By giving freely, you become a more trusted advisor and expert. And this is important - especially when it comes time to make your offer.

So there you have it! The Hero's Journey is a powerful tool to place in your funnel to hook your readers and practically have them begging to buy your product!

So now that we've covered the educational funnel, in the next section, we're going to focus on the sales portion and how to build in scarcity to tip the scales and inspire your readers to ACT.

See you there!

Part 8

- Automated Scarcity - Building the Sales Funnel

Now that you've taken your prospects through the hero's journey and educated them and primed the pump…

… it's time to make the sale.

This part has to be handled with care. You don't want to lose all the trust and goodwill you've built. So you just can't break "out of character" and out of the blue say, "Hey, go and BUY THIS!"

That would be bad.

So to that end, I want to show you how to get this part of

your funnel right. Because after all, this is where the rubber meets the road. This is where all your hard work so far pays off.

In this chapter, we're going to review some tactics that make selling your product a lot easier (like scarcity) and give you points on how to build out the sales sequence portion of your funnel!

So let's dive right in!

Don't Be Cute

The first thing I want to stress is to not be cute about selling.

Often, people are scared to sell! We feel self-conscious that we're asking for money, and the result comes across flat and difficult to understand.

Be very direct and clear. Let them know that you are offering X which will give them Y result and it costs this much. Do not make your potential customer play a guessing game with your sales emails.

How do you get over that self-conscious feeling that some

have when selling? Simple:

Have confidence in your product that you are offering! If it's delivering the value it should, your customer will receive returns that far exceed the sale price.

If in doubt, **Charge More**. You can always charge less later, or put things on sale.

Charging more shows you're confident that you can deliver the goods. Plus, by charging more, you attract higher-quality customers who understand the value of what you're offering.

The converse is also true. If you charge a lot less and cheapen what you have to offer, you'll attract low-quality clients who'll likely end up refunding and giving you a ton of unnecessary hassle.

For a Limited Time...

Another thing you want to make sure you do in ALL your "sales" emails is to create URGENCY.

The best way to do this in your sales funnel is to put an expiration date on when you pull the plug on the offer.

Be very clear with your readers that the offer you are presenting is for a limited time only.

Then, you actually have to stick to it! Many bloggers and online business owners make the mistake of advertising a product for a limited time, but then leave it open for anyone to buy anytime they want. Don't be like the mattress store that's always going out of business; people will lose trust in your message, at which point the scarcity loses effectiveness.

You have to actually put the infrastructure in place to accept orders only for a limited time.. If you don't, and your readers catch on to your bluff, you'll lose a ton of credibility and sales as a result.

So always stick to your guns on this one. Once your offer has expired, that's it. No exceptions, end of story.

This allows you to truthfully create urgency and get people a GREAT reason to buy right now.

More Examples Please!

Now, even though this is the sales portion of your funnel, you want to continue giving real examples of success stories throughout.

You might think that the time for education is done after the Hero's Journey sequence, but it's mission critical to not keep your readers high and dry. Keep providing anecdotes, examples, case studies, and customer quotes that show the success that your customers have experienced using your product.

Why continue to do this? Because people LOVE stories about people like themselves. Just like with the Hero's Journey, they want to hear that someone just like them did just what they want to do.

So the more you can weave these in, the better.

A Helpful Tip...

A helpful tip when it comes to case studies is to create an indexed document full of as many testimonials as you can collect. Call up every customer you've ever had and collect a variety of stories.

If you don't have any prior customers, search and search

until you compile a long list of case studies of a similar nature.

Try to have a story for every applicable situation you can think of.

The reason is, you're going to get a ton of emails like this:

"Hey Keith. Your product sounds really great, but I'm just a single mom in Nebraska and I just don't think this product applies to me."

Or

"I'm just a dentist in Idaho and I just don't think this product applies to me."

People believe that their situation is so unique that no generic advice is able to help them. That's why a variety of testimonials is so important.

Armed with your document of case studies, you can confidently reply with a thoughtful message showing how someone extremely similar to them executed and was successful.

Sometimes, these are the easiest sales!

So make sure you gather all those success stories, otherwise you're leaving a lot of money on the table.

Messaging

The overall message of your sales sequence should be solving the problem that you primed the pump within your educational sequence.

You're letting your readers know that you have the exact solution they need.

Don't focus so much on the features or flashy bits of your product. Make sure you stay focused on solving their problem, and you'll have a much easier time converting readers into customers.

One great way to do this is to really hammer home the benefits your solution provides, and then explain HOW that will impact their life. Paint an enticing picture of them using your product, and then having their problem solved, once-and-for-all.

Show them what life will be like after - all the stuff and pleasure they'll gain.

The more you do this with each email, the better. Remember, with marketing and sales you want to SHOW not tell. So instead of saying "buy my product it's great, I promise!" ... explain to them how that's so. Explain why your product works so effectively and then walk them through painting that wonderful picture of a problem-free life after they've used/consumed it.

Upsell Offers

Upsells are one of the EASIEST ways for you to increase your sales and revenue.

They are the proverbial "low-hanging fruit" of your business and sales funnel.

Because let's face it - acquiring a new customer is hard (and expensive). So wouldn't it be nice if it was possible to sell them more than one thing at a time, without chasing customers away?

Fortunately, it is — in fact, that's what upsell offers are all about.

When most people hear the word "upsell" they probably think of a McDonald's drive-thru cashier saying, "Do you want fries with that?"

That line has undoubtedly made McDonald's billions of dollars, but that's what we'd call a pre-purchase upsell. For course authors, product creators, and self-funded businesses, trying to sneak in an extra product before you've closed the deal may lead a prospect to hold off on clicking "buy."

So, for these kinds of businesses, what I recommend instead is a post-purchase upsell.

A post-purchase upsell offer happens after the prospect has already completed their transaction… after they have already paid.

This allows you to avoid discouraging them from purchasing that first product, while still creating an opportunity to increase the value of the sale.

Let's look at an example.

John has been scoping out an online course about learning to launch a podcast. He's decided to take the plunge, and purchase a course from PodcastingBeginner.com (a fictional site, made up entirely for the purpose of this example).

He adds the course to his cart and goes through the process of checking out. After entering his credit card information and clicking buy, he's greeted with a thank you page — and beneath a message that says "Thank you for purchasing Launch a Podcast in 30 days" is a note asking him if he'd like to add on a package of 6 interviews with professional podcasters, each making $5,000 or more from podcasting each month — a series full of tips and best practices to help new podcasts do the same, which usually sells for $250 or more — for an additional $100.

That is a post purchase upsell offer. **And when done correctly, it's a bit like printing free money. In fact, on average, they generally increase revenue by around 30%.**

So let's take a look at why they work.

Using Psychology to Make a Second Sale

I'm fond of saying that Marketing is just applied Psychology. So let's look at the psychology of WHY post-purchase upsells work so well.

Imagine for a minute that someone knocked on your door and asked you to place a large, gaudy sign reading "Drive Carefully" in your front yard, practically blocking your house. You'd probably laugh in their face — you might even slam the door.

Yet in the mid-1960s, psychologists Jonathan Freedman and Scott Fraser did an experiment that led 76% of homeowners included in the study to agree to exactly that. The experiment was designed to look at what most salespeople consider "getting a foot in the door" and what is more properly known as the consistency principle.

The concept is simple enough: **people want to make decisions that are consistent with the decisions they've made in the past.**

Robert Cialdini talks about the concept in some length in his book, *Influence: The Psychology of Persuasion.* We try to be consistent because doing so is a survival skill — it gives us a helpful shortcut. We think about something once, and then never have to think about it again.

Which means that when the consistency principle is triggered, decisions are made almost automatically.

So, how did Freedman and Fraser get 76% of homeowners in their experiment to agree to have a large sign placed in their yard?

They had a volunteer stop by a few weeks before making the request and asked those same homeowners to display a smaller, three-inch sign that read "Be a Safe Driver."

And, in case you're thinking people back then were just more willing to do things for the greater good than folks are today, there's one more fact that I've left out.

Like any good experiment, Freedman and Fraser also had a control group. For this second group of homeowners, they only made the second request — going straight for the larger ask of the billboard in their front lawn. Their success rate? A much smaller 17%.

I think you'll agree that that's a pretty dramatic difference… and that the consistency principle is a pretty powerful tool.

Getting to Yes: Using consistency in your upsell offer

Of course, putting the consistency principle to work for you, and creating a successful upsell offer isn't quite as simple as just slapping up another product and calling it done.

As with all things in life, there are some things that are more effective than others. In my experience, there are three post funnel upsell concepts that work best.

Upgrade at a Discount

Like in our example above about the podcasting course, this type of post-purchase upsell offers another package or product that provides additional value at a discounted rate.

That discount is directly tied to the customer having just made a previous purchase — so you might use language like, "As our thank you to you, we'd like to offer you a discount on…" and then name the item you're offering as an upsell.

This is the same strategy as the "Super-Size" strategy used at McDonalds in the 90s. For a LOW, LOW price, you can get even more!

Upsell a Subscription

In this type of upsell funnel, the customer purchases a product (or maybe a few products), and you offer them a recurring supply of goods or services for a monthly fee.

Think buying a printer, and having the manufacturer offer to send you ink anytime you run out, if you pay them a few dollars a month for a subscription service. This is also common with products like dog food… but it's not limited to physical goods.

For those with online courses, this may be access to a forum, a mastermind, or weekly "office hours" where they can ask you questions live.

Selling a Secondary (Related) Product

Finally, the third option for a post-purchase upsell funnel is to offer a related product at its usual price… and that price does not necessarily have to be lower than the price of that first purchase.

You might try to upsell them to a higher level of the course they just purchased, or even sell them on a whole new course that serves a related need. The important thing here is to test your funnels, and use dollars as the key performance indicator (KPI).

One of the most surprising things is that the upsell product doesn't necessarily need to be cheaper than the original product. In fact, we've seen that offering a $1,000 product as an upsell on a $300 purchase can actually bring in MORE revenue than going with a cheaper product.

After all, if you use a $1,000 product as your upsell item, and sell 4 of them in a month that's more profitable than if you use a $50 product as your upsell item and sell 15.

Finally, I want to leave you with the idea that a post-purchase upsell funnel isn't limited to 2 steps. If a shopper says yes, and then says yes again, why not ask a third time?

That said, if they say no twice in a row, I usually recommend sending them to a final thank you page without another product. More than that and they're likely to leave the site… and we'd much rather they stick around and leave the door open for more sales later on.

What's Next?

So now you have your sales portion of your funnel set up to convert and sell!

Your emails are using plenty of urgency and case studies, to help tip the prospect into buying.

You've focused the emails on how your product will help them overcome their problem and transform their life.

And, you've created an awesome upsell that will hopefully boost your revenue by up to 30%.

Which means you're ready to pull the trigger on your funnel, right?

WRONG!

Because we're still leaving money on the table!

What do we do about the people that DON'T buy?

In the next Part, we're going to go over two strategies to employ after your sales sequence to bring in more customers after your product offer has closed and your limited time offer has expired.

Part 9

- The Jerks Didn't Buy - How to Save the Sale

So far, you've learned how to get the maximum number of people to buy from your sales funnel on the first try.

But of course, not everyone is going to buy the first time around, right?

There'll always be a few "duds" who could really benefit from what you have to offer, but for whatever reason, they didn't buy (the jerks!).

So what is a savvy business owner or marketer to do?

Do you call them out on it?

Do you send them a special sequence?

Do you put them into another funnel?

Not to worry, I've got you covered.

Read on and learn how you can "save" the sale...

In this lesson, I'm going to show you two tactics for salvaging sales after you've gotten to the end of your sales funnel's open-card window. These strategies are effective and will give you a small additional bump in sales.

Remember, our goal here is to maximize conversions and get as many sales as possible. So these two strategies are the "cherry on the cake" that is your sales funnel to give it every possible advantage for sales success.

Downsell Offer

The first tactic I want to cover is the downsell offer.

This offer will often capture some sales from customers who are interested in your product, but might not have the budget right now or are not ready to commit to the investment of your product yet.

The downsell offer works like this – you're going to offer

one of two things at a lower price than your core product, either:

- A "lite" version of your product. This could be a condensed version of your premium product, or may have some of the extras and bonuses removed.

OR

- A smaller, thematically similar product to your core product.

Both of these downsell offers accomplish the same goal: they offer the value the customer is looking for, just in a smaller and cheaper package.

And what you'll often find is that customers who purchase your downsell offers and receive their value come back and beat down the door to buy your main product!

Here's how I like to do it in three steps:

1. Wait a day or a week after the sales offer closes. Don't attempt a down-sell when they're still in a "No, I'm not buying this" mindset.

2. Send an email with an offer that's different from the one they originally rejected. It doesn't have to be complicated – just use your common sense.

a. Like I mentioned earlier, if the customer declines buying a top-shelf version of your product, offer the lower-shelf version.

b. If they selected from several products, maybe they couldn't decide where to start. Offer them your introductory product.

c. Wait a few days, then send one or two additional emails to remind the customer of the offer. You may just see some of your lost customers coming back to take advantage of your downsell!

3. One other thing to keep in mind: don't come across as desperate and downsell every time someone decides not to buy. You don't want to downsell the same customer multiple times, or they'll undervalue your product.

Last Chance Offer

The second tactic I want to cover is the Last Chance Offer.

Two weeks after the initial product has closed, you'll make one last offer to purchase your product at the price it was offered during the sales funnel.

The Last Chance Offer taps into the psychology of the readers who feel like they missed out, and it gives them one more chance to act and purchase your product! An act of redemption!

The positioning here in your messaging is critical. Do NOT blame the reader for their inaction. That's a quick way to get an unsubscribe.

Instead, approach the messaging like this:

> "I've been getting a ton of emails over the past few weeks from people who wanted to join or buy, but couldn't for whatever reason. So I've decided to offer this product for another 24 hours!"

Again, DO NOT blame the reader. Simply offer this as an unexpected bonus. You'll be surprised how many purchases this simple offer will bring in.

So there you have it - two tactics to pick up extra customers at the end of your evergreen funnel.

Implement BOTH of these strategies and you'll see a big boost in sales!

Part 10

Five Things
to do Right Now

The issue I always have with marketing and business books is that while they're chock-full of strategies, examples and suggestions on how to improve your business, rarely do they present a checklist of *what to do next*.

When finishing a webinar, conference talk, or consulting call, I like to end with **next steps**, the most important things that you can do in order to improve your marketing.

So, based on what we've learned in the previous 9 sections, let's look at the next steps that we can implement to improve our marketing campaigns.

Thing #1 - Choose a campaign to optimize

What I want you to do right now is to choose one (and only one) of your marketing campaigns to optimize. Don't look at two. Or three. Or four. Pick **one** to focus on improving.

Oftentimes marketers will try to do too much at once. They often think that if they're going to optimize one campaign, they might as well optimize all of them.

Resist that urge.

While optimizing your first campaign you'll make mistakes and find more efficient ways to organize your marketing campaigns. If you try to work on multiple campaigns at once, not only will your focus be split, but you won't be able to apply the things you learn to your other campaigns.

Even if we *know* we need to focus on one thing at a time, it can be challenging in practice.

A few months ago I was working with our customer support team to record some videos. I mentioned that we should do one first, so that we understood the process, and could correct any errors before we went too deep into the weeds.

But the temptation to "knock a bunch out" was too great, and the team recorded 10 of the videos right away. It was only after recording all the audio did we realize that we couldn't get the audio and video to sync up. And that the UI and the scripts they had written were slightly different. Additionally, once they started editing them together, we realized that it would have been easier if they had recorded differently, and we could all *totally* hear that lawnmower in the background.

Suffice it to say, we spent much more time redoing all 10 videos that they would have taken to work all the issues out on a single video first.

All of us make mistakes. And that's great, because that's how we learn. It's much better to realize and fix mistakes when they're still small, instead of after you invest hours going down the wrong path.

So do yourself a favor, choose **one** campaign to optimize.

Thing #2 - Find the holes in your funnel

So, now that you've chosen your **one, singular, individual** campaign, we're going to work on understanding how the campaign is currently functioning.

Using a piece of paper, map out the major touchpoints and decisions that a lead can make as they go through the campaign. Touchpoints should not be so specific so that every email is considered a touchpoint, but not so broad that you don't have any definition to the campaign.

I generally define a touchpoint every time a lead makes a decision to engage or not engage with the funnel. For example, we would have touchpoints for: when the lead opts in, when they identify if they are a freelancer, copywriter (or don't tell us), when they register (or don't) for the webinar, and finally when they purchase our product, upsell, downsell or last chance offer.

In the end, it might look something like this:

	A	B	C	D
1	Touchpoint	Leads	Customer	Revenue
2	seq-eg: Optin − PDF			
3	seq-eg: Optin − Checklist			
4	seq-eg: Identify − Copywriter			
5	seq-eg: Identify − Designer			
6	seq-eg: Webinar − Register			
7	seq-eg: Webinar − Attend			
8	seq-eg: Webinar − Stay			
9	seq-eg: Webinar − Miss			
10	seq-eg: Webinar − Replay			
11	seq-eg: Purchase			
12	seq-eg: Upsell			
13	seq-eg: Downsell			

Now that we know what our top-level touch points are, we want to make sure that we're tagging, or somehow identifying, if each lead in our campaign is performing those actions.

Unless you've worked on optimizing these funnels in the past, there's a good chance that you're missing some (or all!) of the touchpoints that you want to be tracking. And that's just fine!

Now, take those touchpoint tags (the ones you already had, and the ones that you just added in), and write them down in a spreadsheet, in the same order they occur in the campaign. We're going to use this in the next step.

Finally, we're going to create an **optimization funnel** from those touchpoints.

In your CRM, find the number of leads who have entered the campaign in the last 90 days, and how many of them have accomplished each of the touchpoints in the funnel. This will give us a list of how many people perform each of the touchpoints as they go through the funnel. Then, put the percent of leads that have performed each action (Touchpoint Leads * 100 / Total Leads).

This lets us know two things:

First, what percentage of people perform each action in our funnel. This lets us know where people are falling out of the funnel, or are losing interest in what we're promoting.

These are the touchpoints that we want to work on improving.

Second, where our funnel gets so narrow that we can't efficiently optimize. As I mentioned earlier, it isn't an effective use of time to optimize your sales page if you're not getting any optins. And it doesn't make sense to optimize your landing page if you're not getting any traffic.

I find that you need at least 100 leads for any given touchpoint before you can begin optimizing. If you have any touchpoints that have less than 100 leads over the last 90 days, that's going to be your first optimization point.

If all of the steps in your funnel have more than 100 leads during the last 90 days, congrats! Now, after you've popped the champagne (or Dr. Pepper), find the touchpoint that has the greatest dropoff in leads compared to the previous step.

This is the touchpoint that we should focus on optimizing next.

Thing # 3 - Find Under-Performing Cohorts

Now that we know the overall performance of each step in our campaign, we want to shift gears slightly and focus on each of the **cohorts** in our campaign. Within your leads, find an aspect of your leads that you can track to differentiate how different cohorts perform through each step in your funnel.

In our previous examples, we used the fact that users identify as either a designer or copywriter. However, a cohort could be something more generic, such as where a lead comes from (their lead source) or which lead magnet or optin brings them in.

Once we've identified at least 2 different cohorts, we're going to get the **lead value** of each of those cohorts.

You get the lead value by dividing the number of contacts in a cohort by the amount of revenue that cohort generated.

In our copywriter and designer example, we'll divide the number of contacts with the "copywriter" tag into the amount of revenue those contacts generated. Then we'll do the same with our "designer" tags.

Now we know which cohort - copywriters or designers - are more valuable in our funnel.

If there are cohorts that are clearly not performing when compared to the average, that gives us a decision to make: We can either cut that cohort out, and stop focusing on them, OR we can see where that cohort is falling out of the funnel, and try to improve that conversion rate.

To improve the conversion rate of those underperforming cohorts, let's go on to the final step.

Also, if you want a full guide to how to calculate the lead value for your cohorts, you can check out our free guide, here: https://segmetrics.io/bonus/calculate-lead-value/

Thing # 4 - Optimize Your Cohort Conversion

At this point we've identified our poorest performing cohorts, as well as the top-of-line conversion rates for both the campaign as a whole as well as each step in the funnel.

Now, in order to optimize that cohort, we're going to follow that same calculation from **Thing #2**, but restrict it to JUST this cohort. So, we'll want to see how many leads we have in each step that have BOTH the cohort tag, and the touchpoint tag.

We'll compare what percentage of the total leads goes through each step, and identify where the number drops off when compared to the average.

Once we have those numbers, we'll have a table like this:

	A	B	C	D	E
1	Touchpoint	Leads	%	Cohort	%
2	Total	1000		500	
3	seq-eg: Optin – PDF	800	80%	400	80%
4	seq-eg: Optin – Checklist	700	70%	345	69%
5	seq-eg: Identify – Copywriter	500	50%	500	100%
6	seq-eg: Identify – Designer	500	50%	0	0%
7	seq-eg: Webinar – Register	300	30%	50	10%
8	seq-eg: Webinar – Attend	200	20%	40	8%
9	seq-eg: Webinar – Stay	100	10%	20	4%
10	seq-eg: Webinar – Miss	100	10%	10	2%
11	seq-eg: Webinar – Replay	250	25%	20	4%
12	seq-eg: Purchase	50	5%	5	1%
13	seq-eg: Upsell	20	2%	1	0%
14	seq-eg: Downsell	20	2%	1	0%

We can now see which touchpoints differ significantly from the average, and identify those touchpoints that don't work for the cohort. In this case, we see that the copywriters have no interest in the webinar, which is our biggest converter to sales in the funnel.

We probably should change the name of the webinar from "How to be a great designer, even when your copywriter is worthless" to something that resonates more with the copywriter cohort.

Part 11

Wrapping It All Up

At this point, you've got the foundation you need to go out and build a marketing and sales funnel the RIGHT way.

You've learned why funnels are so important to your business.

You've discovered how an automated evergreen funnel can free up your time, give you greater profits, and help you scale MUCH faster, while working less.

You now know all about proper tagging, segmentation, and how to think about your list and audience, and the metrics you'll need to track in order to practice Kaizen - the art of continuous improvement on your funnel.

You understand how to turn visitors into leads with an optin magnet.

You know how to take those leads on a hero's journey and prime the pump so they'll be receptive to your sales message.

And finally, you've learned how to actually make them an offer they can't refuse and get them to act now and overcome any procrastination they might have towards buying.

Of course, we've scratched the surface here … as this book's purpose was to give you a foundation from which to build from.

My hope is that you'll take this information and implement it and go deeper into learning each aspect of what makes a high-converting funnel.

And if you need any help in that regard, my team and I are here to help.

Feel free to read the numerous free articles on our site at: https://segmetrics.io/.

And if you want someone to just do it all for you or 1-on-1 help to guide you through any stage of the funnel-building process, feel free to reach out at keith@segmetrics.io.

It's been my sincere honor and pleasure taking you on this journey.

I hope our paths cross again soon.

Keith Perhac

Founder, SegMetrics

Conclusion

Effectively building and optimizing your marketing campaigns is straightforward, but rarely easy.

Marketing is a process of continuous improvement, and the key is to focus on understanding the entire flow of your campaign, but measure improvement on individual blocks, and not try to fix everything at once.

When running a business, you have to make hard decisions about where to invest your time and effort. The same is true in marketing – when you try to focus on everything at once, you'll end up not being able to focus on anything at all.

In marketing, there are a lot of moving parts, even through a relatively simple campaign, and it's tempting to just look at those top-line KPIs. That might be fine in the short run, but it's the outliers – both the good and bad – that help you improve your marketing, and grow your business.

Let's make it happen!

Additional Resources

If you're serious about building a sales funnel that takes paid traffic visitors and turns them into leads and customers automatically, then I don't want to leave you hanging!

That's why I've assembled a list of resources that can help you continue this journey and get you to a place where you've got a great, high-converting funnel that gives you greater profits and more free time.

Enjoy!

SegMetrics Tool Guides

I've put together a free set of tools for your marketing that you can download at segmetrics.io/bonus/book-funnels-that-convert/

- 4 Critical Metrics Hiding in Your Marketing
- How to get the Real Lead Value of Your Optin Magnets
- Building a Quiz That Converts
- Quick-Start Guide to Better Sales Sequences
- Ultimate Tagging Blueprint

I also recommend the following resources for improving your marketing and sales:

- *SPIN Selling* by Neil Rackham
- *Ultimate Sales Letter* by Dan S. Kennedy
- *How We Decide* by Jonah Lehrer
- *Getting Everything You Can Out of Everything You've Got* by Jay Abraham
- *Copywriter's Handbook* by Robert W. Bly

About the Author

Keith Perhac is the founder of SegMetrics, and principal of Develop Your Marketing. In 2010 he left his salaryman career in Japan to employ his marketing and technical skills working with startups and digital marketers looking to grow quickly.

When he's not working on SegMetrics, Keith draws and attempts (futilely) to spend more time outdoors. He lives in Portland, Oregon with his wife and two daughters.

For more information about Keith, you can find his personal page at KeithPerhac.com, on SegMetrics.io, or reach out to him on Twitter: @harisenbon79

Printed in Great Britain
by Amazon

63295814R00070